into oblivion

Into Oblivion

INTO OBLIVION

A ROMANTIC, UNIVERSAL COLLECTION
OF POETRY

by

CHLOË FRAYNE

Dedicated to all those souls
floating through the infinities
of someone's oblivion.

And
to Bridgett, for letting me know hers.

Thank you to Bridgett, Alison, Leya, and Jamie,
for the places you hold in this book and my heart.

3,

2,

1...

Love is a falling upward.
A boat out to sea.
A rocket breaking cloudlines.
An astronomer with
their eyes on the stars.
An astronaut
floating through them.
An understanding
that we carry infinities.
A timeless
and beautiful journey
into that oblivion.

This is the story of her.
Or, more accurately,
the beginning of the story
of what it is like
to love her. :

To witness a miracle is to gaze
too long upon the sun: Suddenly and
irrevocably, everywhere you look
and everywhere you turn and
everywhere you go, you can see
shadows of the miracle out the
corner of your eye – sunspots
pockmarked into your vision to
remind you that something is missing;
something is less; there is more
to the universe than the ordinary -
that somewhere out there waits your miracle,

and it cannot ever be unseen.

This is a paperback love letter.
This is more heart
than words.
This is turning my miracle
upside down and
pouring pouring pouring.

They told me to be careful
with love;
always, careful.

I'm going to tell you
something different.

Be reckless.
Love is reckless.
Give it everything you have
and everything you are
or don't bother.
Be open. Be brave.
Throw caution to the wind.
It doesn't have to make sense.
It's a risk.
You're a risk.

But all the best things are.

And I would endure
a thousand nightmares
for the chance
to dream of you.

I have to be
comforted
by the idea that
if I could give
so much
to someone
who didn't want me
then I must have
so much more
to give
to someone
who does.

Write to them;

to the ones who whisper
to your soul
in the dead of night
with the voices of the stars;
to the shadows that dance
in the corners of your eyes
and haunt you with an
inexplicable need to find
the bodies that cast them;
to those undeniable people
with their futures tied to yours
and their fingers
pulling the string.

Write to them
so they know
it ends with you.

If they tell you
you are worthless,
please know that
your worth cannot be measured
by anything they know.
No, it cannot be quantified
by your bank balance
or your number on a scale
or the people who have hurt you.
You are not a reflection
of the things that you own
or the people you have known.

No, you are a collection
of the things that you value
and you are the only one
who gets to decide
what they are.
And your worth can be found
buried beneath your eyelids
and traced across the palms
of the hands you have held
and scratched upon your bones
by the goodness and the chaos
and the beauty of your soul.

I have always
found comfort
in the earth,
for I know
someday
it will claim me
even if
nobody else
ever did.

So I buried it
with hard hands
in the soft earth
of my heart
and watered it
with whispers
that
patience
is a virtue
and it will grow
only
if I do.

We lived in a world
of ravens and comets
and things that made us
believe
that something
dangerous
and beautiful
was on the horizon.

(And it was)

This is the day
that everything changed.
This is a beginning
that never belonged to an end.
This is my miracle;
a blooming in winter.
This is the most natural thing
I have ever known -
a hello;
an undeniability;
an all-consuming
immediate
falling into place.

(And, oh,
how tangled
and absolute
you feel.)

This is a lift-off.
A struggle.
Hope.
Growing pains.
An ache
in your heart.
Engine-fuel desire.
A burst of courage
against the letting go
of solid ground
and
a fearless,
reckless,
leap.

(I look at you and
the engines have started.
You smile at me and
the ground gives way.)

I believe there is
an oblivion inside us.
that curls and unravels
in love, and a soul.
It is endless, unexplored;
an infinity in your chest.
The way gravity
holds together; pulls apart,
like a blink over galaxy eyes.
The way a universe
expands and contracts,
like a body; like a heartbeat.

We open to one another
and I have only just begun
to learn what you carry
but I believe
that love is as much
a falling upward
as a falling in.

We were caught
in beginnings;
where uncertainty
brings vulnerability
and the question mark
that follows 'forever'
keeps us up at night.

We spoke
like we were trying
to figure out
whether our words
tasted more like
whiskey or vodka.

In the end,
we were just drunk.

This is me,
trying to write
about something
other than you.

This is me,
trying to convince myself
to want something
other than you.

This is me,
failing.

They ask me about you sometimes -
about us.
They want to know
what our lives
would look like if
there were not oceans
spilt between them.

And I don't have an answer,
but I have a plane ticket.

This city
is the most beautiful
in all the world,

because you are living
somewhere
inside of it.

Like autumn leaves
I will rake the earth
and the heavens
to gather
all the shooting stars
I wished for you upon,

and I will use them
to build you
a kingdom
of come-trues.

I can't walk casually
into a restaurant
or make eye contact
when I'm complimented
or reach for your hand
with a stillness in mine,

but I will hold it forever
and whisper my secrets
as I run into your oblivion,
and I will look you dead
in those galaxy eyes
when I tell you I want you,

and for that?
Fuck,
I am brave.

And so I
sat myself down,
stroked my hair,
wiped my face,
held my hand,
and said

"You are okay."

It was maddening.

I felt her
but couldn't touch her;
had her
but couldn't hold her;
and loved her
but couldn't keep her.

I speak to you
like poetry;
I speak to you like
I am writing our story.

You were so special,
and my hands were
so used to slipping,
and I just could not
imagine
holding your attention.

I have bolted shut doors
out of fear
you weren't on
the other side of them.

What I am trying to say
is that
you can fuck up
your whole life
by making decisions
for two people
based off the feelings
of one.

Hope is the most dangerous
thing in the world.

And I wish I could tell you
how it is bundled up
in my chest
and tangled up
in you.

We held it
for what it was:

a promised adventure;
like a wildflower
waiting
to erupt
from the earth.

When I look into her eyes
I see pieces of the stars,
and I cannot help
but wonder
who owned the sky
that stole the rest.

And if we are tied
to one another
by some invisible rope,
then you can
bet your life
I'd throw myself
down a mountain
if my body weight
would pull you
up the other side.

I would thwart
the broken enemy
of Time
to get to you;
fly across fear
and the quaking stars
with my compass
pointing home
and my sights
set on you;
fly
with courageous abandon
and an infallible faith
that these wings
are carrying me
to a place where
they will no longer
be needed.

The truth is that
I have imagined it
a thousand times:
I am standing
on a sun-lit street
and I look up
and you are smiling at me
and for the first time
I know what it is
to be seen by you.

And as much as I do not want
to admit it,
I am so terribly caught up
in the promise
of it all.

I felt the way
her fingers
touched mine
like they were
a door
she was afraid
to close
and I thought,
"there are gentles
to be found here."

Loneliness
looks good on you,
but, like
everything else,

I will strip it away.

Perhaps
those who guard
their hearts
more fiercely
are simply
waiting
for a better kind
of thief.

I do not blame you
for not being ready.

This is what I tell myself.

You were scared.

I cannot hold it against you
for acting like
a cornered animal.

(I just wish you could have seen
that I wasn't the one
boxing you in.)

They tell me
to build my walls
and man my defenses
and when I refuse
they tell me I am brave
but the truth is that
love is not an attack
and to keep you out
is not a victory.

Every brick is an enemy;
every inch a war.

We listed our flaws
like a game;
placed trust
into safe hands;
told to one another
the things that might
have changed our minds
and despite it all,
still saw perfections.

I want to be more to you
than just a collection
of regifted words
playing less insistently
behind your teeth
than they did before
the first time
they spilt through them.

I want you to wake up
at 3a.m.
and understand that
to reach out and touch me
is to learn a new language

and I want you
to reach anyway.

There is a moment of stillness
after you pick up the phone.
I hear your voice and I think how
I would silence the birds;
break all the record players;
quiet the world
for the simple pleasure
of the way you say my name.

- and this
is the good kind
of addiction.

Atmosphere

People are miracles,
and we have to
believe
they can happen
to us.

We held
fireworks
like bombs;

I was
the chemist
with clumsy hands
and you
were the match.

Do you see? -
miles pour across miles
like the scattering
of stars
and still,
I am not afraid.

(and I think
this is softness;
this is strength.)

As far as
I can tell,
you haven't
figured out
what you want yet.

And, me? -
all I have
ever wanted
is your certainty.

I know that we
are an epic love story;

I just don't know
if it is
a fantasy
or a work
of non-fiction.

Maybe I'm not
what you want;
I'm just what
distracts you
until you get it.

But I hope you
still want me
when you aren't
lonely.

I cannot help
but want you
with gasoline soul
and lit-match certainty.

Which is to say,
don't reach for me.
Which is to say,
don't reach for me
unless you know
what you want
too.

She wakes my brain up
like coffee and cocaine
and that feeling you get
lying on a quiet street
on a warm summer night
with the stars above you
and Someone by your side.
She is everything alive
and she makes me feel like
maybe I could be, too.

The only secrets
we keep
from each other
are the ones
we have not
yet learned
to ask for.

I am afraid.
Not of your infinities but
that I am not worthy of them.
You see,
I love you so fearlessly
but choke on explanations.

And you are an inhale
in early morning light.
You are soft petal rain.
You are impossibly worthy
and
I want you
I want you
I want you.

It is perhaps
the rarest thing
in the world
to love
and be loved
in equal measure.

It is perhaps
the hardest thing
not to be.

Maybe we are afraid

(but we are getting
closer and closer and
closer
to being brave.)

What a miracle it is
to wrap my hands
around happiness
and still,
after all this time,
know how to hold it.

If waking up
next to her
doesn't feel like
it's Christmas morning
and you unwrapped
your greatest gift
the night before,

you're wasting her time.

I have always been
attracted
to artists and tattoos.

There is just something
so damn beautiful
about a person
unafraid
of forever.

There is a madness to us;
a drunkenness;
an addiction
like no other;

and I have never known
this fullness,
this overflowing,
this bursting at the seams.
And it is a madness, you see?
It is a high.
It falls from my chest
and plays across my face
and spills from me
in poetry
and I cannot hold it in.

They say
"You talk about her
like she's in the room."
and I smile I smile I smile

with such unbearable light.

I have watched the boats
sway against the sea.
I have noticed,
with great purpose,
the spaces between the stars.

What I am trying to say is that
distance is a concept
that we have given weight.
What I am trying to say is that
when it is faced with love,
it is an irrelevancy.
What I hope you understand
is that I would cross it
in any measure, to be with you.

A soul is a performance
of curling infinities
behind ribs; against bones;
between breaths.
Feel the galaxies in your lungs;
the way such small things
can carry eternities.

There is an oblivion
beneath your skin.
And I do not know
how far it will go;
how long it will last;
but I fall through it
as I learn you and
I am not afraid
because
I do not feel lost at all.

Look at this great big world.
Look at the way it holds you.
The way you fit so perfectly;
take up just enough space.

It's some kind of miracle, don't you think?
That this body of yours
can hold love;
can hold a universe;
can carry you.

You are such a small thing
but you smile
and I think
the fabric of the universe
bursts at the seams.

Look at everything outside you
and, still,
there is so much more inside you.

Say what you will
about insomniacs;
I happen to appreciate
a person
who has clocked
more hours
with the stars.

She was
the kind of beautiful
that could fill
Central Park
with stopped feet
and love notes
written
on autumn leaves.
She was
soft curls
and lullaby lips
and hands
made strong
from holding on
and

she never asked
for attention,
but still
she demanded it.

What a tragedy
it would be
if you were
too afraid
to love me.

Some days
I am all impatience;
all nerves
and hornet nest chest
and anaphylactic heart.
Some days
I drag my feelings
along fence lines
just hoping
you'll figure it out.
Some days
I cannot swallow pride
or bury fear
or find it in me
to reach for you
at all.

Something quiet happens
in the time it takes
to want someone
and to reach for their hand,

and it is the fear
of the reach
and the bliss
of the take
which makes
the space between

paradise.

Know that
as I drop my gaze,
raise my chin
lift my eyes
and find yours,
I am trying to let you go.

Know that
I have tried
failed
waged wars in attempts
to see you in a new way.

And as I fold my hands
unfold
fold again,
know that
I just want to hold your hand.

I had always
been drawn
to the ocean

(and you
had always
been
on the other
side.)

But in this silence,
don't you feel me?
Like a dream you
can't quite remember;
like fingerprints against
the back of your hand.

Give me a love
that uncurls my soul like
petals to the sun
or do not give me
anything at all.

I open to you, like
butterfly wings
to the sky.

And this is
the sunlight.
This is the way
it feels like
your skin.

So here I am;
all of my doubts, all
my insecurities, all
my best and worst
moments and all
the beautiful things
I feel for you
are laid out
at your feet.

Your move.

I wish I could believe
that your hands
were governed
by the face
of a clock.

– *timing.*

I am sorry
for these years spent
with worlds between us;
sorry it has been
Time's hands
that have held you
and not mine.

But every step
I take now
is toward you
and I swear to God,
this time
I will be ready.

It is on days such as these
that it seems
the world has failed.
People must be hurt and brokenness is beautiful
and I appreciate that, I do.
But when I think about you being hurt,
it doesn't seem beautiful at all.
It seems tragic.
Tragic that flowers can be trampled
and stars can wink out
and rainbows can disappear
in the blink of an eye.
Tragic that good hearts
are broken
far more often than bad;
that the boot still crushes
and the darkness still engulfs
and the clouds still reclaim the sky.
Tragic that a person like you
understands how that feels.

Perhaps it is naive
to promise you that
I will never leave you
in some capacity,
but I can promise you
at least this:
I will never leave you
with a head
full of questions
and no-one
to answer them.

I have always been called
too much; too intense.
You are a lesson that
their words were only ever
an unmet need.
And this is a home
for an ocean.
This is a wanting
in equal measure.
This is sunlight
between two flowers
opening.
This is the way
you look at everything inside me
and say you are not afraid.

Tell me a secret
so deep
you can feel it
scraping
against your bones.

Drop a bomb
so catastrophic
it could shatter
the foundations
of everything
I think
I know about you.

Tell me the things that scare you.
Let me love you anyway.

If you came here
with any intention
other
than for me
to love you
spectacularly,
you have set us up
for
tremendous failure.

I cannot help but feel you
in the breeze between
these buildings that have held you,
like you are
etched upon their walls.
And this place feels like you -
has seen you and
touched you and known you
in ways I never have -
and when I am here,
I cannot help but walk these streets
drunk
on the possibility of you.

This city knows your secrets;
this sidewalk knows your name.

I have counted
the moments
I've wanted you
on my breaths.

(and you're coming closer)
(and I'm breathing faster)

How absurd that
they ever tried
to value you
by what they found
on your surface.

I will say this much
of myself:
I have never been one
to hesitate
at the shore.

And did you feel? -
how the whole world
fell into place
when I realised
I want you
with me
when I see it.

Kármán

You are the moon
and I am the sea -

do you understand?

I rise
and fall
for you.

This is the line in the sand;
the brink of falling;
a point of no return;
a breath before breaking clouds
and a romance
in the way our skies
spill into oblivion.

This is the edge
of every possibility
I ever dreamed of.

I always fall in love
accidentally;
like too-big shoes
on too-small feet;
like words that trip me.

(I am sorry I have not learned
to stop apologising
for earthquakes
and gravity.)

I love you like
coming back to life.
I speak to you like I'm
coughing up dirt
and you smile at me
like you know
what it is
to unearth bones.

She was one of those people
on the verge of
something remarkable;
struggling, yet undeniably
destined for greatness.
One of those people
dancing on the precipice
of love,
with a fast-approaching dawn
bringing success, and a sun
that would know nothing
of her face but a smile
that would never again
quite fade away.
One of those people
who curls inside your soul
the moment you meet
and makes you pray to God
you might just be that greatness
they were destined for.

I've been thinking about love letters;
how they usually start with
your name.

There is an almost unearthly goodness
in loving you.
I hear it in the grass
and it whispers only
of the way your legs brush against it;
I see it in the sunlight
as it plays against your hair;
I feel it in the quiet
when the city is stretched beneath us
and your heart beats by my side.

And I keep thinking,
how could anything I write to you
be anything but a love letter?

I will not settle
for anything less
than the way I feel
when I look at you.

It was in the way
her hands
always sought something
to hold onto,
and I always watched them,
hoping they'd find mine.

There is courage in the way
I throw open doors.
Trust is a padlock
and I am a house
with a skeleton key
and you are on the doorstep
and we are
open open open
and there is nothing
holding you here
but
I want you to stay.

The way you smile gets
stuck in my head
like a projector
playing slides
on the back of my mind.
Yes, that machine lights up
the moment your face does
and I am glued
to the screen 'cause
I can't get enough.
And there you are
in front of me
and I am smiling
like I am in love
with the fact
that I
can make your face
look like that.

It is on days like this
that every mile,
every flight
and every fucking inch
is the goddamn enemy.

It's all about
who you want
when you're drunk;
when your hands
won't stop shaking
and your mind
has lost hold
of everything
but a name.

Perhaps it is not
to be encouraged,
but to me, there are
few things more flattering
than a good drunk text.

You know that feeling
when you are
outstandingly drunk
and even in
the infinite haze,
you can't forget them?

"You are on my mind
even when it is obliterated.
You are on my mind
even when I've lost it."

God, it's beautiful.

I just hope
I learn
to let go
as beautifully
as the day does;
to surrender you
gracefully
to different skies.

She was a collection of moments
I couldn't let go of;
infinities curled inside infinities.

And she folded them
into my hands
to teach me that
holding on
doesn't have to hurt.

It came with the realisation
that breaking a heart
is often
not
an act of malice;
for hearts are heavy things
that cannot be given back lightly,
and have an unfortunate habit
of slipping through
unpractised fingers
and ungentled hands.

And they fall even faster
and harder
than we do.

Love me in a way
that frays me
at the edges,
scratches at
my button eyes,
tugs the stuffing
from my chest,
and teaches me
that broken things
seldom become so
by being left
on the shelf.

Oh, this is what it feels like
to love in equal measure.

You talk about me
and I write about you

and we both forget to breathe.

I don't know how
to tell you
that you are
so intimately tied
to every idea
I've ever had
of love.

I cannot say
goodnight
to you
without
falling in love
with the idea
of morning.

I will watch you crumble
in the summer;
water you with whispers
of your worth.

I will see you fall
in the autumn;
catch you with moonlit hands,
like leaves.

I will bury you cold
amongst the stars
in the winter;
wrap your hands around them
to keep you warm.

I will watch you rise
with the flowers
in the spring;
tell you how I loved you
with the seasons;
tell you how your petals
still fall like walls;
tell you what a miracle it is
to bloom.

She looked at me
like I was
a star
she wished
would fall.

So I did.

And it's the same way
you don't know
it's raining
till it
hits the ground;

this falling.

I will write about you
forever.

You are simply choosing
in which tense.

Here is the truth of it all:
I have hidden my love away;
carved hope upon my bones;
lined coat pockets with
our somedays and
stayed warm all
these winters apart;
wished for you
in dandelion fields
and still,
found myself wanting -
still, in our darkest corners,
felt my breath whisper
the light of your name.

I have not
(have never been)
a patient person.
Rain rolls down
the window and
I will it
to fall.
But time was of
such
little consequence
with you,
for you were never
a fleeting thing;
never as fickle
as the weather
or as temporary
as cold glass.

And even when you were,
I was in awe of the journey.

I will never forget the day
I told someone you were mine
and ever so quietly
you said
"I can be yours."

(And I hope you
never forget
that it's true,
and I think it
all the time.)

All of a sudden,
I am afraid
of a life lived without you;

of scraping the cusp
of oblivion
with my somedays
still
wound through my hair
and pressed between my palms
like a prayer
and no way to see
what it would have felt like
to grow old
with your eyes
watching me.

He told me
I could have found
people like you
anywhere, and
I needn't have ever searched,
and all I could think about
was how wrong a person can be.
7 billion people in this world
and I have come in contact
with enough of them to know that
what exists inside you
cannot be found in anyone else.

You are not interchangeable;
you are irrevocable,
you are unique in all the world,
and you are mine.

If you ever desire
to question
your beliefs,

fall in love,

then ask yourself
if they exist
by something
so unspectacular
as coincidence.

And I wonder
if you hear
how peacefully
my breath surrenders
to the sound
of your name.

At best,
I was
hopelessly
in love with you.

At worst,
I was
completely
unaware of it.

And isn't it beautiful?
This love;
this coming undone
at the thought of you.

There was something
about her
that rattled the stars
in their cages.

There was something
about her
that set us all free.

There is only one kind
of distance
between us
that matters,

but

how much simpler
this life would be
if only Fate
had tied us
together
with a shorter string.

These lights
are off, and
oh,
how beautiful
the darkness
would be,
if you
were here
with me.

I asked
to know her,
and she just
smiled
and dug
six feet deep;

a little grave
beside her,
just for me.

We fell in love
the way the stars
come out at night:

the sun slid
across our hands,
the day took
its last breath,
and
ever so quietly

our skies
came back
to life.

And it's getting harder,
isn't it?
To quiet that feeling
late at night
that tells you
I should be there.

If they stare
(which they might),
knot your fingers in mine and
do not think of white flags.
If they talk
(which they will),
tell them that this love
didn't come easy;
how it rained on that night
when we couldn't sit still.
And even
if it hurts us
(which it could),

know that I am not afraid
to hold your hand.

As much as I
have tried
to deny it,
I think
if I were to
fold together
all the things
I have ever wanted
the infinity
of it all
would still look
an awful lot
like you.

The company

of stars

You smile at me
and, oh,
this is more
than survival.

I am sorry, sorrier
than I can ever tell you,
that anyone has ever
made you believe that
what you hate about yourself
should be hated,
but I must tell you this now,
and I hope you will believe me.

You are not beautiful
the way other people are beautiful.
You are beautiful
the way
the stars are beautiful,
and there will always be those
who are afraid
of the immensity, of the light.
But there will also be
astronomers,
stargazers,
and me.

We come alive
in the presence
of things
that make us feel
like we must
exist
for a reason.

Life is just a story -
do you understand?
Love
is a certainty
that even if
you are not
on every page,
you are on
the last one.

I don't know how
to look at people
like I'm not
in love with them
and I don't know how
to love them
like the best moments
of my life
aren't when
they're looking at me.

You see,
I would
unravel myself
forever
just to wrap
around you
to keep you
warm
for the
winter.

We were teacup vodkas
and bottles wrapped in brown paper bags.
We were alcohol and secrets
poured through lips that felt their buzz
in equal measure.
We were confessions whispered
and buried safe beneath the carpet
of brothel walls
that had heard far more than our own.
We were voice memos at midnight
and stories told on New York streets
with different accents and held hands.
We were written upon Wilmington walls
with a certain electricity
and scrawled across stars
that sung insistently
that I had been searching for something
and this was it –
this was it
and you were it
and I should never let you go.

I'm struggling
to find the line
between
what I would
and wouldn't do
to be with you.

I look at you
and see exploding stars
and sunlight through treetops
and ice creams melting
on summer sidewalks
and you look at me
and see flesh and features
and all things ordinary.

I look at us
and see fireworks and adventures
and an ever-thwarting of time
and you look at us
and see today
with a sort of separation
from tomorrow.

You love me like a person
and I love you like a miracle.

I will let this go
like an idea
that fell asleep
before I could say
Goodnight;
before I had a chance
to blanket it in love,
kiss its eyelids
in the moonlight,
press my breath upon
its ear, and whisper
that it was
the sweet dream.

Love
is the only thing
in the world
that can make you feel
as though you are both
the strongest
and weakest person
in it.

What an honour
it is,
to be held
gently
by a savage.

When they looked at
bird cages,
they thought of
bad things
like captivity
and clipped wings,

but they ornamented
her life
because
they reminded her
of her past
and how
even featherweights
can break steel bars
if only
they have their sights
set on the stars.

Love and space
are quite the same
in their infinities,
you see?

Even butterflies
feel like meteor showers
if it's the right person
setting your sky on fire.

Still, I know that I
reach for you
too much

(not with words but
with growing pains)

Still,
everything piles up
and breaks down
at the sound
of your name.

Listen:
I am avalanche heart;
split-seam desire;
stranger to subtleties -
do you understand?
This is just
another rooftop
I'm shouting from.

To love
is to stand
in the biggest crowd
imaginable, and still
beyond all reason,
look for the face
of a person
you know
isn't there.

Make me believe
I'm good for you
or enough for you
and maybe

I'll believe
I'm both.

Make me believe
you want me
as much
as I want you

and I'm yours.

I do not want to be
just another person
in your procession;
marching out
I-LOVE-YOU's
in a chorus line
of clichés.

I want to love you
so fucking tremendously
that I
am the only one there.

See, I am the one
with my hands on the wheel.
I have packed suitcases
of sacrifice
into the trunk
with picnic blankets;
filled the gas tank
to the brim
with desire;
removed all the mirrors,
accepted the risk;
burned the roadmaps
and forgotten your name.

We are nothing
but grown-up children
searching for a new,
more permanent way
to tell the world
the same thing
we scrawled upon it
when we were young:

We were here.

I know this journey
has not always
been beautiful, but
don't you see? -
the way this darkness
claws and snaps and
lies to you;
the way it forces you
(with both sword and shield)
to fight for yourself;
the way it teaches you
you are worth the war.

It's not always perfect.
It's not always soft,
or gentle, or painless.
But it's always easy.
Which is to say,
I wake up every day and
it does not take
anything
away from me.
Which is to say,
I could not help but love you.

And still, I choose you
in every way.

Everything changed for me
when I realised that
every step I take
is either
toward you
or away.

We uncurl
in this quiet
without unravelling;
it is an art.
Stretch our backs
against the sky
and feel sunrise
touch our skin
and wonder
when the noise
will begin.

Do you see me
in the garden? -
I am burying insecurity.
I look back
over my shoulder and
when I catch sight of you
I think,
"This time I will feel worthy."

I go back to staring
at the earth
over my seeds;
go back to praying
they will sprout
anything
but weeds.

I hope you know
I see you.

I hope you know
I am never
looking away.

In truth,
there are oceans
inside me
for you;
great
and terrible
storms;
mountains
moving like
avalanches
set off
by the sound
of your quietest breath.

Every day, I ask the world
to take care of you; to keep you
safe and well and whole,
and remind you that
you are not alone
even when you feel it.
I do not ask this of the stars:
they are even farther away from you
than I am, and like people,
never fall at the right time.
But sometimes I will ask the moon,
for I know she is awake
in the hours that you are.

I hope this world
is watching over you
in all the moments
I am not.

I blamed an ocean,
so I crossed it

(hands like waves)
(heart like anchor)

but planes cannot close
all distances,
and words cannot sustain
all sails.

She asked me
if I felt
like I would ever
feel at home,
and I thought of you
and told her
that the only time
I feel like
I'm in the right place
is when I'm with the people
who carry it
inside of them.

Lay with me here
on rooftops;
laugh
in this quiet
so I might know
what it is
to be
in the company
of stars.

If it is very dark
and I am very still
and there is nobody
to hear the sound
of my bones
scraping the sky,
maybe it will sound
like music;

maybe the night
will still smile
against my skin;
maybe
you will, too.

There is something to be said
about the way a person can grow you;
can change you; push tools against your hands
and teach you how to garden
all that is inside you.

And if people bring you butterflies
when all the work is done,
remember that
you are the rose.
You are the garden.
You are the whole damn reason
they are there.

I watched her
the way
an astronomer
watches the stars:
with a light in their eyes
and a feeling
burrowing through their soul
into the pit
of their bellies
that they are staring
at every possibility
in the universe.

I remember once that
someone told me
"The universe does not
pay that much attention"
and I thought of her
and said
"It does to some people."

I remember thinking
how beautiful it is
to notice a human
for all these little things
they do.

(And how sometimes
it is impossible not to)

and

the way she blushes.

I was afraid -
didn't I tell you?
I wanted to reach for you
a thousand times
but I was stilled
by the idea
of worthier hands.

I wanted to tell you
how there is an almost
unbearable tenderness
in me
for you.
And I was afraid.

But could there not
be bravery here?

Here is the idea:
we empty our hands
of fear;
wash them clean;
wrap them
unapologetically
around what we want;
call this love
what it is:

courage.

It was just
you and me
and that feeling
that nothing else
would ever be
enough.

She scattered the stars
like breadcrumbs
to lead us home

and I followed
through galaxies,
planetary orchestras,
asteroid seas,
and eternity;

until humanity
felt like nothing more
than a story
told to us
by oblivion.

Oblivion

There is a gravity
inside us,
don't you think?

A pull.
An undeniability.
A falling into place.

A quiet understanding
in the way
I see you
and the ocean makes sense.
A moon falling into orbit makes sense.
The way the universe
is held together
makes sense.

In all honesty,
loving you was
a rewilding
of my heart

and it does not
come back
when I call it
home.

And there is your smile

(and this is
an admission
that with you,
I never
stood a chance.)

I hold forevers
in my palms
and I must
remember
not to wrap them
around
temporary people.

Show me the sky.
Raise your hands
to the clouds and
tell me how
they are holding you.
Look between
the stars and I
like you understand
what it is
to be human.
Know that
in the vastness
of these infinities,
I see you
in the same way.

In my final hours,
before the veil
of the infinite
has been lifted,
and I am standing
at the door
of my Somedays
with my story
tucked safely
in my back pocket,

I will speak only
of you.

The rest of the world
is just
a background
behind you.

Forever is just
a promise that
if your soul exists
in any reality,
I will find it.

Fate
is an understanding
that I have before,
and will again.

In 100 years,
it will still be
just the beginning.

- *this is the nature of forever.*

It is impossible to doubt
the goodness
and the magic
of the arcane universe
when it has granted us
this miracle
of existing
at the same time.

There is a place inside me
that exists just for you.
I have struggled
(with too many words)
to give it a name.
It unravels,
and I think
it has no end
and, God,
it is an immeasurability
that I do not understand;

but it feels like fate,
and I am so madly
in love with it.

I searched her
for signs
of the infinite;
signs of immortality;
signs of supernatural.
- for she couldn't
be human.

She just couldn't.

I fell in love with her
for the way
she looked at the stars:

like she belonged with them.

And, God,
she looked at me
the same way.

I just hope
there's
a part of you
that only
breathes
when you
see me.

When this world has forgotten
how to be quiet -
how to open its mouth
without bombs falling out;
When it is all sharp edges
and you are all soft heart
and it has forgotten
how to hold you
without tearing you apart,

know as it wraps itself
around you that
you are a reminder
that a part of it
still remains soft;
know that you are teaching it
a better way;
know you are a part
of gentling this world.

We are
but specks
upon the eyeglass
of Time,
praying
he has a greater
patience
for unclean things
than we do.

When I think of our future,
I do not imagine us
as a little old couple
holding hands
in a nursing home.
I imagine us as ghosts,
sitting in a cemetery
on some bitch's grave,
scaring the shit
out of people
and telling stories
to the stars.

I do not imagine
a mortal life
for an immortal love.

They tell me that I am lucky
to have found you and
had our fleeting oblivion...
and I am. I am.
But I am searching
for the people I belong with
and if this is them, then
I do not want an hour
or a minute or a night,

I want a lifetime.

I love you like
seasons.

I hold you
the way the earth
holds a flower
and
I would not
blame you
for leaving
with the rain.

She was a rose;

they were just
glasses.

We had forgotten
the art
of delicate things;
forgotten the practice
of gentle hands,
soft words,
and fierce extremes.

And your heart?
It took us all
by surprise.

In truth,
your beauty
could never be
my favourite
thing about you;
for it is bound
to this century,
and I intend
to love you
for much more
than one lifetime.

Close your eyes tonight
and I will tell you
that story
about the moon;
how we stay up
all night
telling stories
about you.

My fingertips
grazed your soul
and nothing
ever felt
the same
again.

How obscene
that this world
will not end
with you; that
there will be a day
that goes by
without you,
and the fabric
of the universe
will hold steadfast
at the seams,

and I will fall apart
alone.

It feels like forever,
doesn't it?
Like words on paper,
like breath on skin.

Some days I feel safe;
secure; I understand you.
Some days it is as simple
as the way you
answer the phone.
Some days it is more complicated.
Some days I spend every minute
reading into what you say
and everyone I see
looks better for you than I do
and I am afraid afraid afraid
that you see it, too.

But even on those days, little flower,
I love you like breathing;
like a hand on a heartbeat;
like it is the easiest thing
in the world and
the only thing
that has ever made sense.

When I am old
and time has opened up
and spilled out
my memory,
I will lie
on my deathbed
reading our story
to the sky

and it will be
the only one
I have left
because it will be
the only one
I never stopped telling.

Can you imagine
a love like that? -
A certainty
so absolute
it does not falter
in time?

In truth,
before you,
I wouldn't have
been able to.

And now?
Now I don't need to.

How tirelessly
I have listened
to the sound
of the universe
crumbling away
around us
every time you speak.

It's some kind of tragedy,
don't you think?
How our eyes
slide over beauty
when it becomes
too familiar.

It's some kind of love,
don't you think?
How you still catch my eye
after all this time.

I cannot tell you
the nature of fate,
only that it is found
in the coming and going
of planets;
the pattern of the stars;
the way there is a hush
against the ocean
but a crashing joy
when a seashell chest
finds the courage
of a pressed ear.

We will not have
a happy ending.

(We will not end)

If there is a gravity
inside me
(which there is),
if there are universes
and constellations
and a quiet oblivion
(which there are),

loving you
needs no explanation.
Losing you needs no explanation.
The push and pull
of knowing you
needs no explanation.

It is a breath.
It is an eternity.

Oblivion
is standing at the edge
of the sea.
It is a different level
of infinity.
A weightless
all-consuming
moment of fear.
An emptying of pride
and insecurity.
A heart wrapped
seamlessly
around hope.
A full,
unbearable
smile
from someone you love.

And, oh,
what an honour it is
to know yours.

All I know -
all I have ever
needed to know -
is that
if you offered me
your hand,
I would take it.

How beautiful it is -
this place where
our souls live.

I say
"There is an ocean
between us,"
and she says
"I don't feel it."

I hope this world has
examined you closely;
mirrored with grace
the sound of your breath;
spent lifetimes
learning your eyes and
traced maps of the universe
against your skin.
And I hope, after all of this,
it whispered to you
that your greatest beauty
uncurls like magic
beneath.

I am sure
I have loved you
for infinite lifetimes

(but I think
this one
is my favourite.)

I have met you
in my dreams
for what seems like
an eternity.
I have seen you,
always,
in Parisian streets.
I imagine a day
when the morning comes
and I'm with you;

and I would show you
all the ways
a little rose
has grown me;
and I would tell you
what an awakening it was
to love you;
and I would know that
with you,
I am as close to oblivion
as I have ever been.

In the end,
maybe it all
comes down to
the last story
we tell
and the person
we tell it to.

And in the end,
when I whisper
our story
to the stars,
I hope you're there.

Explore this world
so completely with me
that someday when
other planets ask
of home,
we will know
how to intimately
describe it.

(You will speak
of Earth,
and I will speak
of you.)

It was the best part
of my life,
loving you;

and after,
I spent the rest
of my days
telling stories
of how far I fell
into oblivion.

into oblivion.